Hospital Visitation Handbook for

Bonny V. Spearman

Hospital Visitation Handbook for Ministers
Steward Publishing, Union, New Jersey

Spearman, Bonny V.
Hospital Visitation Handbook for Ministers /
Bonny V. Spearman
Includes bibliographical references
ISBN 978-0-9796106-0-8
ISBN 0-9796106-0-5

Printed in the United States of America

The paper used in this publication meets the requirements of the American National Standard for Permanence of Paper for Publication and Documents in Libraries and Archives 239.48-1992.

Dedication

To my mother

Contents

Acknowledgements

Special thanks to Father, for Your love and enduring grace. Thanks to my family for your invaluable support and encouragement. Thanks to Pastor for timely inspiration.

Preface

"For I was an hungered, and ye gave me meat: I was thirsty, and ye gave me drink: I was a stranger, and ye took me in: Naked, and ye clothed me: I was sick, and ye visited me: I was in prison, and ye came unto me [...] In as much as ye have done it unto one of the least of these my brethren, ye have done it unto me."

Jesus Christ

It is possible, albeit quite plausible even to consider that there is something special to God about caring for those who are suffering. In all of our spiritual endeavors and pressing toward the "mark", as mentioned by the great Apostle Paul, we realize that reaching the "high calling" of which the apostle speaks, ultimately requires the losing of our lives for Christ's sake. As God's workmanship, created in Christ Jesus and thoroughly furnished unto good works, we walk holding dear the requirements of faithfulness and love, which we demonstrate by keeping the great commandments. We are our brother's keeper. "Pure religion and undefiled before God and the Father is this, to visit the fatherless and widows in their affliction, and to keep himself unspotted from the world" (James 1:27).

Jesus, the first born of many brethren and our ultimate example, visited the sick and the dead. Moved with compassion, Jesus interrupted (or so it would appear) many of his journeys to minister to the infirmed in body and soul. Often Jesus approached those who could not see Him and those who dared not even petition Jesus' grace. Bowed down, broken and weary, some had all but given up the fight. Today, Jesus calls out to them, through us, to be loosed from their infirmities.

Introduction

"By the sick, I do not mean only those that keep their bed, or that are sick in the strictest sense. Rather I would include all such as are in a state of affliction, whether of mind or body; and that whether they are good or bad, whether they fear God or not."

John Wesley

When visiting the sick, you will encounter believers and non-believers alike. You will encounter lovers of Jesus and haters of God. You will meet Christians who are joyful and Christians who are disappointed, disillusioned, depressed and full of despair. You will stand at bedsides and look into sullen eyes that question God's faithfulness. Peace filled believers will encourage you as they march toward death's door. Yet, at times you may witness suffering beyond the ability of any human to comprehend. You will long to caress children, whose frail bodies curved with disease, shame complaining hearts. Eyes will fasten upon you as saints and sinners search for answers. Are you up to the task? If you answered, "Certainly not," you are right and perhaps ripe for the undertaking.

As in antiquity, contemporary gates of Bethesda encircle many who are resigned, reconciled and resolute to live with illness and disease while hope fades by the day, month, year and decade. John Wesley aptly reminds us that affliction knows no boundaries of beliefs, proximities, status or character. It is our assignment, therefore, to look beyond the outward appearance to behold the image and likeness of God and to remember how precious each of God's creatures is to Him.

Jesus is the healer, the burden bearer, the only deliverer of grace unfathomable and the supreme author of peace. We are merely His messengers. We go as ambassadors, representing the King of all Kings, to extend Jesus' arms in love to those for whom He shed His precious blood. We refrain from judging and condemning. The Apostle Paul asks, "Who is he that condemneth? It is Christ that died, yea rather, that is risen again, who is even at the right hand of God, who also maketh intercession for us" (Romans 8:34).

Remember, God sent not His Son into this world to condemn the world, but that the world through Him might be saved (John 3:17). Let us, as students of the Holy Spirit, eagerly set aside our inclinations and subdue our notions and emotions. Let us discipline our discernments to rather discover the limitless power of God's love and mercy toward His creation.

Let us, therefore, walk in the Love of God and leave the proving to God alone. Let us walk in the expectancy of God's mercy and grace that heals. Let us walk in meekness, considering our own selves, lest we fall, lest we offend. Let love prevail. Love never fails. Love melts hearts and soothes fears. Love assures and reassures. Love is kind. Love empathizes and sympathizes. Love accepts. Love speaks and love keeps silent. Love prays so that all present can understand. Love defers to wisdom. Love defers to itself.

Scriptures for Healing

"Surely he hath borne our griefs, and carried our sorrows: yet we did esteem him stricken, smitten of God, and afflicted. But he was wounded for our transgressions; he was bruised for our iniquities: the chastisement of our peace was upon him; and with his stripes we are healed."

Isaiah 53:4-5

"Bless the LORD, O my soul, and forget not all his benefits: Who forgiveth al thine iniquities; who healeth al thy diseases;"

Psalm 103:3

"Beloved, I wish above all things that thou mayest prosper and be in health, even as thy soul prospereth."

III John 2

"The Spirit of the Lord is upon me, because he hath anointed me to preach the gospel to the poor; he hath sent me to heal the brokenhearted, to preach deliverance to the captives, and recovering of sight to the blind, to set at liberty them that are bruised."

Luke 4:18

"And the prayer of faith shall save the sick, and the Lord shall raise him up; and if he have committed sins, they shall be forgiven him."

James 5:15

"And Jesus went about all the cities and villages, teaching in their synagogues, and preaching the gospel of the kingdom, and healing every sickness and every disease among the people."

Matthew 9:35

"Jesus Christ the same yesterday, today and for ever."

Hebrews 13:8

"Who forgiveth all thine iniquities; who healeth all thy diseases."

Psalm 103:3

"Heal me, oh Lord, and I shall be healed; save me and I shall be saved: for thou art my praise."

Jeremiah 17:14

"For I will restore heath unto thee, and I will heal thee of thy wounds, saith the Lord;"

Jeremiah 30:17

"He sent his word, and healed them, and delivered them from their destructions."

Psalm 107:20

"The centurion answered and said, Lord, I am not worthy that thou shouldest come under my roof: but speak the word only, and my servant shall be healed."

Matthew 8:8

"Is any sick among you? let him call for the elders of the church; and let them pray over him, anointing him with oil in the name of the Lord. And the prayer of faith shall save the sick, and the Lord shall raise him up; and if he have committed sins, they shall be forgiven him."

James 5:14-15

"Who his own self bare our sins in his own body on the tree, that we, being dead to sins, should live unto righteousness: by whose stripes ye were healed."

Peter 2:24 I

Part One

Preparation

"And I sought for a man among them that should make up the hedge, and stand in the gap before me..."

Ezekiel 22:30

"Love is intercession on its knees..."

Karen Walden

Hospital Visits Begin At Home

Hospital visits begin with your private prayers for the sick. As you spend time in prayer, earnestly intercede for those who are suffering illness. According to Isaiah 53:5 and 1 Peter 2:24, healing is God's will. The scriptures in 1 John 5:14-15 and Isaiah 55:11 assure us of the integrity of

God's promise to keep His word. Seek the Lord for His Spirit of grace and anointing as you prepare to visit the sick.

By God's grace, God may use you to minister healing to many. Always remember Psalm 115:1,"Not unto us, O LORD, not unto us, but unto thy name give glory, for thy mercy, and for thy truth's sake."

Visiting patients in the hospital is a divine privilege that God has allowed you to have. When visiting patients, keep in mind the following procedures for etiquette, respect and safety. In 1 Corinthians 14:40 the apostle Paul teaches that God is the author of order.

The Importance of Prayer

Before beginning and at the conclusion of a hospital visit, always pray for God's covering and protection. As you begin your visit, pray as well for God's anointing to provide His guidance in your choice of words. The Lord will prepare your heart as you seek to be an instrument of His love toward those you visit.

It is important to pray at the conclusion of the visit to refresh your spirit and remove any feelings of oppression or heaviness before returning to your home or office.

Anointing With Oil

Anointing with oil should be done with the permission of your pastor and the patient, or patient's family. Many patients welcome the anointing with oil. However, for those who have yet to either understand or prefer the anointing of oil, God's healing still prevails. Remember, it is the prayer of faith that shall save the sick (James 5:15).

Displays of Emotion

Hospitalized patients are in need of your faith, support and encouragement at all times. Sudden illness, serious or prolonged illness, accidents, and unexpected life changes can produce the effects of fearfulness and anxiety in patients. While it is natural for you to feel empathy and compassion for those who are suffering illness, note that patients can sense fear, nervousness and alarm from those who visit. What patients really want and need from you is calm assurance. Patients want to believe that God's love abounds for them and that His presence, healing power, and will to heal remains.

It is essential to maintain your faith and composure at all times. Patients will look to you as source of confidence and strength, even in the direst of conditions with the gravest of prognoses.

If You Are Sick

When patients are in the hospital and suffering from illness, their immune systems, in many cases, have become compromised and are weaker. If you are suffering from a contagious illness, such as a cold or flu, please refrain from visiting patients until you are completely well. In this way, you will avoid exposing patients to harmful germs and bacteria, which could aggravate their current condition.

Part Two

General Protocols

"Wisdom is the principal thing; therefore get wisdom: and with all thy getting get understanding"

King Solomon

Patient Information

Before visiting the hospital facility, call patient information to confirm that the person you are planning to visit is there and receiving visitors. Depending on their conditions, patients may be moved, undergoing tests or procedures at various times during their hospital stay.

Clergy Identification

Be sure to carry your clergy identification to the hospital with you. Clergy identification distinguishes you as one visiting in an official capacity to pray and offer spiritual comfort.

Parking

Always park in designated public parking areas and obey all hospital parking regulations, including leaving fire lanes free for emergency vehicles and those being discharged.

Many hospitals charge for parking. However, with clergy identification, security may allow you to park without a fee. Upon entering a hospital facility, check with security to have your parking ticket validated. Have your clergy identification ready to present. Without it, hospital security may decline to validate your parking ticket and you may have to pay for parking.

Note that there are some facilities, such as state hospitals, that may not have a procedure in place to validate parking for clergy. It is a good idea to check with security before parking in a fee area.

Hospital Visiting Hours

Hospitals impose specific hours of visitation in order to maximize time for patient rest and recuperation. Visits, although welcomed, can be tiresome to patients and for this reason, hospitals regulate certain hours of visitation. It is their way of ensuring that patients benefit from specific uninterrupted periods of rest. As a minister, it is your duty to demonstrate respect for all hospital regulations and the patients you visit. Most hospitals allow regular visits from 11:30 AM until 8:00 PM daily.

Note that the visiting hours for maternity, pediatric, critical care, intensive care and psychiatric units may vary. If you are visiting someone in a specialized unit of the hospital, obtain information on visiting hours before venturing to the facility.

The only time that a minister should attempt a visit in any unit outside of the regulated times is if there has been a severe emergency and you are specifically called by the patient, the patient's family member or the patient's nurse or physician to respond to the hospital right away. This is rare and usually occurs only with senior pastors.

Obtaining Visitors' Passes

After entering the hospital, go to the patient information desk. Wait your turn and ask for a visitor's pass to see the particular patient you are there to visit. You may be asked the purpose of your visit. If asked, respond by saying that you are clergy there to visit briefly with the patient. You may then be asked to display your clergy identification and directed to sign in a clergy roster, which is usually located at the patient information desk or held by security. In almost all cases, you will be able to obtain a visitor's pass.

On occasion, you may be told that all of the passes are out and that you have to wait until someone else who is visiting returns. If you know the patient is expecting you, you can call the patient's room and, without requesting someone to leave, let the patient know that you are there. The patient may indicate that another visitor is leaving and ask you to come to the room. If not, you may decide to wait or return at another time.

It is important to understand that security and information desk personnel have discretionary rights that permit them to disallow visits by anyone whom they believe is disobeying hospital regulations.

Hand Washing Procedure

Hand washing is an essential requirement for visiting patients. There are restrooms and hand washing stations available for this purpose. Please observe the following procedure for washing your hands.

1) Retrieve a paper towel
2) Use the paper towel to turn on the water at the sink
3) Wet your hands with warm water
4) Leave the water running

5) Lather your hands with soap

6) Rub hands together thoroughly, cleansing your hands and wrists for 15-30 seconds

7) Rinse your hands and wrists

8) Retrieve a fresh paper towel

9) Dry your hands and wrists

10) Use the paper towel to turn off the water

11). Discard the paper towel

12) If in a restroom, use a fresh paper towel to handle the doorknob and open the door

13) Discard the paper towel

Hand washing should be completed before and after visiting each patient.

Observing Universal Precautions

Universal precautions are practical infection control measures developed by the United States Center for Disease Control (CDC) to restrict the risk of transmission of blood borne pathogens spread by specific body fluids and blood.[1] More specifically, Universal Precautions are hospital safety procedures designed to protect patients, hospital personnel, and visitors from infection caused by the spreading of germs and harmful bacteria. Universal precautions are to be taken seriously and should always be followed. Utilize the following universal precautions for visiting all patients at all times.

1) Wash your hands before entering any patient's room in order to ensure that you are not bringing germs into a patient's environment.

2) When in a patient's room, refrain from handling patient articles, tables, phones etc. unless asked.

3) When approaching a patient, refrain from freely touching patients unless patients indicate that that they wish to be touched.

---

[1] "Healthcare Wide Hazards (Lack of) Universal Precautions," *U.S. Department of Labor Occupational Safety & Health Administration,* https://www.osha.gov/SLTC/etools/hospital/hazards/univprec/univ.html.

4) Wash your hands after leaving a patient's room and before entering another patient's room.

Patient Privacy

Patient privacy is to be respected at all times. Patients' conditions and diagnoses are personal and are reserved for patients, patients' families and medical personnel only. When visiting patients, refrain from inquiring about the nature of their illnesses, diagnoses, prognoses, or any other private information. This will ensure not only the preservation of patient dignity and privacy but also your adherence to the Health Insurance Portability and Accountability Act, also known as HIPAA.[2] HIPAA was originally enacted in 1996 to protect patient health care coverage with insurance companies. However, in April of 2003, legislators developed The Privacy Rule as a component of HIPAA. The Privacy Rule is designed to limit the inquiry and disclosure of patient Protected Health Information (PHI). Patient Protected Health Information includes, but is not limited to any information about a patient's health status, medical treatments and diagnosis.

[2] "Health Information Privacy," *U.S. Department of Health & Human Services,* http://www.hhs.gov/ocr/privacy/index.html.

Remember, as clergy, you are visiting in an official capacity, which is different from that of a family member, casual friend or acquaintance.

Concern About Treatment

During a visit, a patient may share concerns with you relative to the treatment the patient is receiving at the hospital. On occasion, you may make an observation that arouses your concern as well. In either case, unless you are a member of the immediate family, refrain from addressing the issue directly or confronting hospital personnel. If you believe it is expedient to address a concern, share it with members of the patient's immediate family and defer to the family's judgment in handling the concern from there.

In almost all instances, there are facts and variables that weigh into the course of action (if any) the family prefers to take. Additionally, both the family and hospital personnel may be more informed than you about the patient and the necessary manner of care required.

Food and Flowers

It is quite common for family members to take food items that are sure to bring smiles to patients. Traditionally, visitors have taken flowers to cheer ailing patients as well. In wondering whether to take food or flowers to patients, consider the following.

Often, patients are observing strict diets that preclude the ingestion of certain items like salt and sugar, for example. In addition, there are times when patients are undergoing a series of tests that require fasting for hours or days at a time. When patients are undergoing tests or are in preparation for a surgical procedure, they are often classified "NPO" by their physicians. NPO is from the Latin term, "Non Per Os," which means, "Nothing by mouth." When patients are classified, NPO, they may have neither water nor ice chips for a specified time. Usually at the doctor's discretion, a patient will end this fasting period with clear liquids in specific quantities.

Because diet is such a vital factor in healing and well-being, it is always best to defer to the regimen a patient's physician prescribes. Unless you are a member of a patient's immediate family who is certain of the patient's dietary allowances, it is best to refrain from taking food on your visit. Your good deed could otherwise impede the healing process.

Flowers add beautiful accents to any room and while usually appreciated, at times flowers may be inappropriate. First, many hospital protocols include the restriction of flowers in intensive care units. Secondly, some patients have allergies and other sensitivities that become aggravated by the fragrance and pollen in flowers. Lilies, for example, can be exquisitely pleasing to behold, yet too aromatic to stand, especially in a small or closed room.

Today, people take cards or uplifting reading materials. Friends, coworkers or family members often take balloons or other gift items they know their loved one would like to have close by.

In any case, the most important gift is your presence. Your smile and warmth are all you really need to carry. If you decide you want to take a gift, always consider the comfort and wellbeing of the patient you are visiting as well as any other patients who may be sharing that patient's room.

Part Three

The Visit

" I was sick and you visited me..."

Jesus Christ

Before Entering a Patient's Room

Before entering a patient's room, always check that you have the correct name, room number and bed assignment. In many hospital facilities, patient's names and bed assignments are displayed just outside the patient's door. Because there are times that you may not personally know the patient, this will ensure that you are entering the correct room and interacting with the exact person you are there to visit.

If you are unsure or do not see the name displayed, ask a nurse or nurses aid at the nurse's station to confirm the room number and bed assignment of the patient you are there to visit. It is advisable to make certain that you are at the correct room visiting the correct patient before entering.

Observe the outside of the patient's room to adhere to any postings that may be present. When medically necessary, hospital personnel may post signs requiring that Personal Protective Equipment be worn by everyone entering the patient's room. These postings are referred to as PPE's. Be careful to adhere to all such requirements before entering a patient's room. Most often, the purpose is to protect the patient from outside germs and bacteria brought in by visitors.

As you approach the entryway to the patient's room, gently knock on the door and wait for a response. When the patient answers, state your name and purpose for visiting, always addressing the patient by name. For example, "God Bless you, (Sister or Brother. . . Patient's name), I am Minister (Your name) from (Your church). I am here to pray with you." The patient may then invite you in.

When you initially knock and do not hear a response, it could be that the patient is attempting to dress or prepare before you enter. Wait for a moment and knock again before stepping into the room. If you walk into a room and notice the patient undressed or in the restroom, step back out of the patient's room and assure the patient that you will wait outside until she is comfort-ably dressed or back in bed. Usually, if not resting, the patient can let you know that she is aware of your presence. Assure the patient that you will wait outside until she is comfortably ready for you to enter.

Be willing to leave and return at another time if the present is inconvenient for the patient. Otherwise, wait for the patient to let you know when you may enter the room.

When Hospital Personnel Are Present

If there are hospital personnel present, they are either examining the patient or performing some other medically necessary function. Immediately tell the patient that you will remain outside during their examination. Step back out of the room and wait completely outside of the room and away from the door until hospital personnel have completed their care. You may observe nurses or doctors leaving the room. However, wait until they tell you that it is permissible to reenter.

Sometimes, hospital personnel leave a room temporarily just to retrieve a needed item and return right away. They know you are waiting and will usually tell you when you may reenter the room. Although patients may some-times invite you to remain, always wait outside a patient's room while hospital personnel are present. Preserve and prioritize patient dignity by respecting patient privacy at all times.

Patients in Isolation

When patients are in isolation, it is because they may be suffering from contagious illnesses. Contagious illnesses can be transmitted by airborne or other pathogens. As with all patients, when visiting a patient in isolation, be careful to observe the visiting regulations. You may be required to utilize Personal Protective Equipment, which consists of gear worn by health care workers and others to reduce exposure to communicable diseases.[3]

Personal Protective Equipment consists of gowns, gloves, masks, respirators, eye protection, and shoe coverings. Sample contagious diseases include, influenza (the flu), hepatitis A, hepatitis B, meningitis, pneumonia, strep throat, tuberculosis and, the common cold.[4] If in any way you are uncomfortable visiting a patient in isolation, please refrain from doing so.

Patients in isolation are extra sensitive and can discern your discomfort. This can cause increased anxiety for the patient and embarrassment for both of you. There is nothing wrong with limiting your visits to patient areas that are most comfortable for you. As you become seasoned, you may find your level of discomfort decreasing.

---

[3] "Personal protective equipment," *U.S. National Library of Medicine,* http://www.nlm.nih.gov/medlineplus/ency/patientinstructions/000447.htm.

[4] "Diseases & Conditions," *Centers for Disease Control and Prevention,* http://www.cdc.gov/diseasesconditions/.

If you are pregnant, or nursing, consider conducting isolation visits when you are no longer pregnant or nursing.

Patients in Reverse Isolation

Patients in reverse isolation are in needed protection from harmful germs and bacteria brought in by visitors. Exposure to outside germs threatens to compromise a patient's already weakened immune system. Therefore, visitors are required to wear personal protective equipment, such as gowns, gloves, and respiratory equipment in order to limit the patient's exposure to germs and bacteria.

The requirement to wear personal protective equipment is more often to protect patients from germs brought in by visitors than the reverse. It is important to demonstrate complete compliance with visiting regulations at all times.

Entering a Patient's Room

When entering the room and approaching the patient, smile, restate your name and purpose for visiting. Acknowledge any other family members or persons who may also be visiting the patient. Observe the patient's posture, locations of other visitors, and medical equipment. Walk to the bedside that appears to be most comfortable for the patient. After walking to the patient's bedside, remain standing. Even if invited, refrain from sitting, especially on the patient's bed. Refrain from sampling any of the patient's food or handling patient possessions.

Be careful to look the patient in the eyes and smile lovingly at all times. When patients are in the hospital they may experience feelings of loneliness, anxiety, fear, nervousness, and embarrassment. Refrain from staring at the patient's body or machines. You could further embarrass or alienate the patient by your expressions. Be conscientious of your countenance at all times.

Extend love and greetings to the patient on behalf of your pastor and tell the patient that the pastor is praying for her. For example, "Sister or Brother (Patient's name), pastor says to tell you that he (she) loves you and is praying for you. How are you feeling today?"

After the patient says how she is feeling, ask if the patient needs anything. The patient may ask you to pour a cup of water or place an article close to her reach.

Sharing Scripture With a Patient

Hearing God's word can give birth to and increase patients' faith. As you prepare to read a scripture, first ask if the patient would like you to. If so, ask the patient if she prefers that you read particular portion of scripture. Many patients enjoy favorite passages from the Bible that bring them comfort and assurance. Among them are Psalm 23, Psalm 91 and Isaiah 53:1-6.

When sharing a scripture, read the verses by putting in the patient's name where applicable. Maintain eye contact with the patient as much as possible. This helps the patient to personalize the scripture. Always choose uplifting passages that assure God's love through His words of peace, calm, healing and restoration. When you have finished reading the scripture, immediately prepare to pray.

If the patient does not want you to read a scripture, it

could be that the person is tired, in pain or in such discomfort that she needs the visit to end quickly. Smile and immediately prepare to pray.

Preparing to Pray for a Patient

As you prepare to pray, observe the posture of the patient. If you believe the patient wants you to, ask the patient if it is okay to hold her hand and pray. Patients may sometimes reach for your hand. If so, gently hold the patient's hand (not the one with the intravenous needle in it because this can cause discomfort to the patient). Depending on a patient's posture, you may sometimes lightly rest your hand on top of a patient's hand as a gesture of affection or point of contact. Be mindful that sometimes it can cause pain to patients to be touched. There may be some patients who simply do not prefer to be touched. If you are unsure, refrain from touching the patient.

Always allow the patient to remain as comfortable as possible. Reaching, turning or moving may be uncomfortable for patients. You may have to move to the other side of the patient's bed to accommodate the patient's existing position.

As you position yourself to pray, ask the person if he or she has received Jesus as Lord and Savior (or is saved). If the patient replies affirmatively, proceed with a brief prayer for healing. If the patient says that he or she is not saved, ask if the patient would like to receive Jesus into her heart. If the patient states that he or she would like to receive Jesus, begin the prayer by leading the person to Christ, then pray for healing and restoration.

If the patient is undecided or declines to receive Jesus, assure the patient of God's love for her and still pray for the patient's healing. You are planting a seed that will yield increase as the patient experiences the love of Christ through you and others.

Leading a Person to Christ (sample)

"Father, I believe that You so loved the world that You gave your only begotten Son, that whoever believes in Him would not perish but have everlasting life. I believe that Jesus died on the cross for my sins and was raised from the dead after three days. I repent for my sins and ask You, Lord, Jesus, to come into my heart and be my Lord, Savior, Redeemer and Friend, in Jesus' name, I pray. Amen"

A Sample Prayer for Healing

"Father, in the Name of Jesus, we acknowledge Your presence and thank You for Your love toward 'Sister or Brother (Patient's name)' . Thank You, Father that according to Your word in Isaiah 53:5, 'Sister or Brother (Patient's name)' is healed by the stripes of Jesus and His blood makes her (or him) whole. We thank You that You sent Your word and healed Sister or Brother (Patient's name) and Your word cannot return unto You void. I pray that You grant Sister or Brother (Patient's name) continued rest and complete restoration because she (or he) is Your beloved. Jehovah Rapha, You are the God that heals Sister or Brother (Patient's name) and we thank You for her (or his) healing in the name, which is above every name, Jesus Christ, who is Lord. Amen." Always remember to pray God's word over patients. Remember, Isaiah 53:5 and 1 Peter 2:24.

If other family members or friends are present, ask God's blessings upon them as well.

Patients Who Are Sleeping

If upon gently knocking on the door, you hear no response, just above a whisper, greet the patient State your name and purpose for visiting, "God Bless you, (Sister or Brother. . . Patient's name), this is Minister (Your name) from (Your church). I am here to pray with you." If you still do not hear any response, the patient may be sleeping. Lean into the doorway and wit as few light steps as possible, notice the patient.

If the patient is sleeping, it is because rest is an essential element of healing. In their efforts to recover from injury or illness, patients are sometimes taking medications that cause sleepiness. Refrain from approaching the patient bed because you may wake the patient. Sudden surprise can cause unnecessary anxiety for patients and could make your visit less welcomed. Instead, gently back away offer soft prayer at the entryway of the door, and exit the room. Jesus hears you and though the patient may not be aware of your presence, Jesus is.

Patients Who Are sedated, Unconscious or Comatose

When patients are sedated, unconscious or comatose, it could mean that the patient's infirmity or injury has caused significant damage to the body. At times, patient physicians treat patients with medications that serve to reduce pain. As well, certain powerful medications are used to sedate patients. There may also be times when patients are unable to breathe on their own and are assisted by respirators or other artificial means. In these cases, you may quietly approach the patient's bedside.

Gently place your hand on top of the patient's hand, lean over to lightly whisper in the patient's ear. Tell the patient who you are and your purpose of visit. Remember to extend love to the patient on behalf of your pastor.
If the patient is unsaved or if you are unsure of the patient's salvation, you may lead the person to Christ by whispering the prayer of salvation in the patient's ear. Proceed with the prayer of healing. Tell the patient that Jesus loves her, her pastor loves her and that you both will continue to pray for her.

If other family members or friends are present, ask God's blessings upon them. Extend love and continued prayers from your pastor and you. Gently back away and exit the room.

Patients Who Are Dying

Patients who are dying are often quiet and unresponsive. Some have ceased eating and talking. Family members are often present. Conduct the visit as you normally would. Keep in mind that long after patients have stopped eating and speaking, they can still hear quite well. Anything discussed in the presence of a dying patient, however unresponsive, can likely be heard by the patient.

Gently place your hand on top of the patient's hand lean over to lightly whisper in the patient's ear. Tell t patient who you are and your purpose of visit. Remember to extend love to the patient on behalf of your pastor.

If the patient is unsaved or if you are unsure of the patient's salvation, you may lead the person to Christ by whispering the prayer of salvation in the patient's ear. Proceed with your prayer for healing. Tell the patient and family that Jesus loves her, her pastor loves her and that you both will continue to pray for her.

If other family members or friends are present, ask God's blessings upon them. Extend love and continued prayers from your pastor and you. Gently back away and exit the room.

After Praying for a Patient

At the close of the prayer, assure the patient again that pastor loves her and will continue to keep her in prayer, as will you. Gently back away from the bed and out of the room.

Although the patient may say that she is feeling well patients still need rest. Your visit should be completed in three to five minutes. It takes energy away from patients to receive visits, especially from clergy, because of the formality involved. Be mindful that a word from your pastor coupled with your presence and prayers are encouraging to patients and any strength a patient gains should be preserved.

Upon Leaving a Patient's Room

Upon leaving a patients room, go to the nearest rest-room (out of the view of the patient or the patient's family) and wash your hands. Hospitals carry many germs and airborne bacteria and it is important that you do not carry any home to your family.

Many patient rooms are equipped with sinks. However, refrain from using the patient's sink or cleansing your hands where the patient can see you. Always use a rest-room or hand washing station out of the sight of the patient or the patient's family. This allows you to wash your hands while preventing any misunderstanding or embarrassment to anyone.

Visiting Babies

When visiting babies, be careful to exercise caution, as babies are the most fragile of all human beings. A baby's parents should be present during the visit. As you enter the baby's room, identify yourself and purpose for visiting. Greet the parents, any other family members or friends that may be present and the baby, calling it by name. Express love to the parents and family on behalf of your pastor. Ask if there is anything the parents or baby needs.

As you position yourself to pray, approach the bedside of the baby. Refrain from picking the baby up or exciting it in any way. Refrain from leaning over the baby and breathing in its face. As a sign of affection or point of contact, and with the parent's permission, gently touch the baby on the forearm with one finger (not on the baby's hands) as you begin to pray.

At the close of the prayer, assure the parents again that the pastor and you love them and will continue to keep baby and the family in prayer. Gently back away from the bed and out of the room. Go to the nearest restroom or hand washing station (out of the view of the family) and wash your hands.

Visiting the Elderly

A good listener makes pleasant company for the elderly. Learn to follow their lead when visiting. Begin with your greeting and observe from there. If an elder wants to talk, listen. Another may merely desire company to sit a while or play a game such as checkers. Always ask if there is anything you can do to for them and follow through. God will bless you.

Without promising, try to visit as a matter of routine. The elderly are often lonely and will look forward to your visit. If you miss your visit, the elder may still appreciate your call. For the elderly, consistency and quality matter more than the length of the visit. With every visit, your presence declares, "You are not forgotten."

Visiting the Mentally Ill

Mental illness afflicts people of all ages, ethnicities, professions and religious affiliations. People suffering from mental illness are needful of the same empathy, compassion and careful respect as those suffering physical illness. Because of the nature of mental illness and the stigma traditionally attached to it, patients who allow you to visit extend a valuable and special trust to you. Remember that as with all patients, you are being trusted not to judge.

When visiting the mentally ill, it is advisable to keep the visit brief without appearing hurried. Although appearing joyful at your arrival, keep in mind that a long visit can be distressing for the patient. As with patients who are physically ill, those who are mentally ill may become disquieted in an attempt to accommodate your presence for long periods. All patients need rest, including the mentally ill because exhaustion can occur on every level.

Keep in mind that mentally ill patients may also appear anxious at times and may petition your assistance in any number of areas including, release from the hospital. You may even hear unfavorable allegations of mistreatment. Be sympathetic, yet try to avoid much discourse in any negative vein. Focus the conversation on gratitude, God's love, faith and blessings. Your visit should leave the patient feeling strengthened and encouraged. Endeavor to always leave patients with a smile, both inwardly (as much as possible) and outwardly.

Visiting The Chronically Ill

Chronic illness is infirmity that is continual, persisting, stubborn, seemingly never ending, or reoccurring over long periods. Patients who suffer from chronic illness need consistency in care, prayer and encouragement. Try to visit on a regular basis, as the afflicting nature of chronic illness breeds loneliness and weariness in patients. Consistency and quality matter a great deal to the chronically ill. With every visit, your presence declares, "You are not forgotten."

Two by Two

Consider Mark 6:7. "And he called unto him the twelve, and began to send them forth by two and two; and gave them power over unclean spirits;" Matthew 21:1 states, "And when they drew nigh unto Jerusalem, and were come to Bethphage, unto the mount of Olives, then sent Jesus two disciples" In 1 Samuel 15:22, Samuel asked the question, "...Does the Lord delight in burnt offerings and sacrifices as much as in obeying the voice of the Lord? To obey is better than sacrifice, and to heed is better than the fat of rams." Jesus determined to send His disciples out two by two. It is His lead that we obey and follow.

Consider the apostles, Peter and John, in Acts 3:1-4. "Now Peter and John went up together into the temple at the hour of prayer, being the ninth hour. And a certain man lame from his mother's womb was carried, whom they laid daily at the gate of the temple, which is called Beautiful, to ask alms of them that entered into the temple; Who seeing Peter and John about to go into the temple asked an alms. And Peter, fastening his eyes upon him with John, said, Look on us."

When you have another minister with you, you are ensuring that you witness and share the same experience.

In this way, you are able to watch and cover each other in prayer. Traveling with another also helps to alleviate misunderstands or liabilities. Paul, in Romans 10:2 said of a people whom God loves, "For I bear them record that they have a zeal of God, but not according to knowledge." Although you may be enthusiastic and willing to go alone, always take another minister with you. It is for your protection. It is wisdom. It is God's way.

Proverbs 4:7 teaches, "Wisdom is the principal thing; there-fore get wisdom: and with al thy getting get understanding."

Thank you for reading the
Hospital Visitation Handbook for Ministers

The Hospital Visitation Handbook for Ministers is a companion manual that accompanies the APL Hospital Visitation Training Workshop.

Hospital Visitation Training is a part of the APL Leadership Development Series, which offers in-depth leadership training for emerging, intermediate and senior leaders in many facets of organizational, personal and professional development.

For workshop and training information, to view other publications or to order additional copies of the Hospital Visitation Handbook for Ministers, please contact us at HospitalVisitations.com.

The Hospital Visitation Handbook for Ministers

is also available in Spanish

AplLeadership.com